Quick

Quick

A Pediatrician's Illustrated Poetry

Text by John Graham-Pole, MD
Illustrations by David Crown, MD

Writers Club Press
San Jose New York Lincoln Shanghai

Quick
A Pediatrician's Illustrated Poetry

Writers Club Press
an imprint of iUniverse, Inc.

For information address:
iUniverse, Inc.
5220 S. 16th St., Suite 200
Lincoln, NE 68512
www.iuniverse.com

ISBN: 0-595-23606-5

Printed in the United States of America

Contents

Illustrations

From Original Mezzotints by David Crown, MD

Permissions

The following poems are reproduced with permission of the relevant journal publishers.

Journeys and Sojourns: J Poetry Therapy 5,129,1991; Breaking News: J Amer Med Assoc 267,1004,1992; Bone Marrow Tale: Internat J Arts Med II,18,1993; Consensus and Consent: Internat J Arts Med II,19,1993; Protective isolation: J Med Humanities 14,235,1993; Phase II Trial: Ann Int Med 120,691,1994; Health Care: J Emerg Med 12,407,1994; Waiting: J Poetry Therapy 7,217,1994; Will (as For Will): J Poetry Therapy 7,218,1994; Flowers and Soldiers: J Poetry Therapy 7,219,1994; Fear: J Poetry Therapy 7,220,1994; Victorian Scene: Amer Phys Poet Newsl Fall,12,1994; Eroica: Arch Fam Med 3,938,1994; Requiem (as Requiesca in Pace): Arch Fam Med 4,11,1995; The Color of Grief: J Poetry Therapy 9,131,1996; Signs (as The Sign): J Poetry Therapy 9,137,1996; Dying: J Amer Med Assoc 275,1874,1996; Joy: Lancet 349,66,1997; Leaving Mother: IN Blood & Bone, Univ Iowa Press 65,1998; Intern: J Med Humanities 18,273,1997; Candor: IN Blood & Bone, Univ Iowa Press 27,1998; On the Ganjiang Canal: Pudding Mag 36,34,1998

Foreword

I got a call at two in the morning from a patient's mother. She was mad and she was scared. Mad because I hadn't figured out what was happening to her son; scared for the same reason.

I had been caring for this twelve-year-old since he went down with leukemia earlier in the year. He had received a lot of anti-cancer drugs, more recently a marrow transplant—therapy with the potential to cure, but beset along the way with horrid complications. I had spent much of the past evening at his bedside after he had suffered an epileptic attack out of the blue. The seizure had lasted an hour—a lifetime for this mother. It took massive doses of several medicines to put a stop to it.

He was running hectic fevers—something else I had no explanation for. All our tests—a spinal tap to be sure he didn't have meningitis, a CAT scan in case he had bled into his brain, checks of other immediate things—drew blanks. Good news as far as it went, but no help in dredging up answers to this mother's questions.

When we were sure he had enough medicine on board to forestall any further fits, I did what I could to reassure her that things were in control, that nothing was happening to threaten his life.

It's not so rare at times like these not to have answers. Can you put your fears to rest, get some sleep? The nurses will call me right away if anything else happens.

She heard me in silence. Still with a feeling of helplessness but having no more bright ideas about how I could help either mother or son, I went home to bed.

She spent the next four hours perched by his unconscious body in its lonely bed, the questions twirling about:

What's happening? How can I help him? Is he going to make it? What next? She had to unloose her pent-up questions on someone—and I was the most accessible. Anyway, she told me later, she was mad that I could take off home to bed when she was sure her son could die any minute. Hence the two AM call; the outburst leaping all over me down the line.

Three-quarters-asleep, I did my best to listen; I had nothing more to give. Over the next few minutes I heard the rage turn to tears; a few minutes more and there was sudden laughter coming down the wire. The tension had popped like air from a balloon. After she finally hung up the phone, I groped my way back into sleep, while she groped her way to penning her first poem in twenty years.

I'm Scared[1]
Why do they do this to a person?
You bring them up to behave,
say their prayers, wipe their noses,
then they go and get sick
and scare the willies out of you.
The craziness of kids, scaring us
both like this. He's doing his best,
old doc, I guess he doesn't
know it all after all.
But I don't want him going to school
on my son. God, stop scaring us
like this. And son, read the book
where it says, after the bit
about brushing your teeth
and not eating too much candy
and not staying out late, the bit about
not having fits—and giving us fits.

I call this *therapeutic* poetry at its best. This mother—this "non-poet"—in the midst of her sleepless terrified night had instinctively turned to poem-making's resource, snagging the thoughts that were breaking surface like fish asking to be hooked.

I thought I knew how she felt; I had done the same myself not so long before, knocking out the first poem of *my* adult life to bring back a day years ago during my lowly medical internship. I had failed, and failed again, to lure blood out from the scarred veins of a man my own age.

He had leukemia too. I too was scared and mad. The senior physician had demanded more tests. The patient had been enormous, at least in memory, with veins anyone could surely pierce. All I got for my trouble was a great big blood clot—a hematoma—on his left forearm:

"...blue line on ulnar pulp bulged,
skittered squeamish, coy around my darts
until the time the hematoma sprang
screaming its livid tracer on the passes
of ineptitude, pricked me to sacrilege:
he'll die anyway (they all did then),
the blasphemy of blame: god why this
tiny vessel in this gargantuan frame?" 2

I had no notion this was what I was thinking and feeling that desolate day of my 24-year-old life; nor that it would take *that long*—twenty years—to suddenly see things clear, and to put healing pen to paper. Forrest Gander calls memory *a crumpled map of lost roads crisscrossing body and brain.*3 *Re-membering* means to bring all those missing parts of yourself—your *members*—back. Which is what I was doing, at long last putting myself back together again through poem-making. I'm glad it didn't take this mother as long to come to this blessed resource.

Fear, a poem in this collection, is my own attempt to remember and resolve that middle-of-the-night telephone conversation with my young patient's mother. Where on earth would I have ended up had not poetry swept me up in its arms? William Carlos Williams wrote the first fragments of his poems on his patients' charts while he was about his house calls in Rutherford, NJ. Stick-it notes have done it for me. A line scribbled sitting on a patient's bed on morning rounds finds its way to my journal, thence on to my word processor as a poem's first bare scratchings. And there it is, my honest friend when science makes no sense; what John Keats, a graduate of London University's medical school 150 years before me, surely meant by *the truth of the imagination.*[4]

Acknowledging, ten years ago, my lifelong love affair with words, I passed through a gateway into a garden of resonant, forgiving grace. Many of my poems have become *requiems*, celebrations, of young ones I have known shortly, before they rode, astride their dragons and unicorns, out to celestial summer camps, heavenly places that put life down here pretty much in the shade. Seen from these young souls' view, the work is done; time to go play in the deathless sun.

Medicine is a bottomless well of poems. Ever since reclaiming my voice, I have tried to link it to my work, ground it in the urgencies and mundanities of my practice. Some days the importunities of my own interns, the weight of inexplicable laboratory data, the outcry of angry family members, the daunting competence of Emergency Room and Operating Room nurses, get between me and my penning the definitive truth about health care's predicament and resolution—a Pulitzer for poetry, my ego says. Other days, I can see it clear and egoless: each and all of these happenings *are the poem.*

I spend a lot of time sitting on hospital beds, and clinic examining tables, listening and talking to patients of all ages and sizes. When I listen well—doctoring's art—poems come; from conversations rarely shared in grocery check-out lines. I hear of day-to-day lives in distant towns that are points on the state map; lives of people whose bodies and pathologies I know too well. Hearing these stories is at the heart of service; they are the poems that let me quieten, attend, intuit, love. I call them the *precise subjective* of illness, data that cannot be quantified in the approximate language of science. This undertow, often weighted down beneath the surge of biomedicine, is older and tougher than hospital buildings, or prescription pads, or pills.

Thirty years of service to children has dared me to experiment, to fall on my face a lot. Children have uncovered for me the last and greatest lesson: *souls thrive on failing at bigger and bigger things.* May I never forget the outrageous, elegant, go-for-broke messages, the magical, sweet-as-nuts memories of children. But perhaps I will always wonder—*Where do they go to, these young ones? And where do grown-ups come from?*

Meanwhile, I try through writing poems to lay a finger on the *purpose* of illness, on its pulse. Set down on this terra-formed star half a million years back, blessed with the forever fruit of our earth's crust, it seems legitimate for we human beings to wonder if illness and death—such universally inevitable things—hold gifts for us. Even for those newly ill—who find too many wrappings taped and tied against even the smallest gift within the smallest box within. Of some mysteries only poems can make meaning. Poems turn denial and withdrawal into compassion—*feeling with.* They turn fear into mercy—*thank you.* In their potent blooming, they shape and adorn inarticulate thought; their resonance gives voice to half-swallowed intuition; their guiding hand carries us over a bridge of communication and celebration; their timeless rhythm balances the polarities and synergies of our lives.

1. Reproduced with permission from Graham-Pole, J: *Illness and the Art of Creative Self-Expression,* New Harbinger, 2000.
2. Reproduced with permission from Graham-Pole, J: *Venipuncture,* Annals of Internal Medicine, 120, 691, 1994.
3. Gander, F: *The Measured Word: Essays about Poetry and Science.* Univ Georgia Press, 2001.
4. Keats, J: *Letter to Benjamin Bailey,* November 22, 1817

Florida Dawn

On the porch, my toe knuckles crack their echo to the swamp toads;
the cats prowl between the dim calladia and spider plants,
salute me with their soft brushings. Sulphurous dampness
dwindles before the advancing heat. Crimson punctures the raintrees,
blearing the glimmer of sharp stars. Window squares gleam
from the cater-corner house; the single street lamp glistens on
pine shadows tapering to the lawn, sprinkler spray lighting
grass blades like points of city light seen from a passing plane.

I reverse from the garage, smoke graying my sight line; the car's
rumble rouses early squirrels, scatters puddles from the
driveway's concrete pocks; we sweep past azalea verges on streets
thick with oak mold. In the square, the giant guardian of the
campus gate receives me, authoritative hand raised in greeting,
luring in this conspirator to share the night's events, colossal
armfuls of gestures curved in intricate ballet to play her story out.
Whip-poor-wills join this welcome to my day's transactions.

Morning A-Z

Task A, on rising: clean kitty litter,
leads to task B: find litter bag;
diverts me to utility room and task C:
load sheets in washer, but first task D:
heft wet tees, socks, undies from washer
to dryer, and task E through G: add Tide
to washer, Bounce to dryer, turn on both;
back at last to B: locate litter bag and scooper
under flung towels, pausing for task H:
empty dehumidifier's water tray onto
Mother-in-law's tongue, and task I:
transfer folders, texts and laptop from
car to office; so back to bathroom and
almost forgotten A, after a break for tasks J
through S: ten slow and deep ones, then task T:
supplement the washer's load with a Persian
runner Bluebell has mistaken for the litter box;
finally, finally, to kitchen for tasks U through W:
grind beans, add water to percolator, turn on.

Oh, and the afterthought of tasks X through Z:
find pen, paper, pen this poem.

Home

For two years we slipped
into the tiny interstices of time
between patients, publications,
presentations, peers,
the raising of a many-angled house
amid the does and turkeys
at the northern reach of town.

Before we slew a stem or sunk a hole
we paced its foundations thirty feet
further west, to gain the shelter of
a grove of magnolias, oaks, offering
sacrifice to the household gods
of one five-year-old loblolly
where our front door stands.

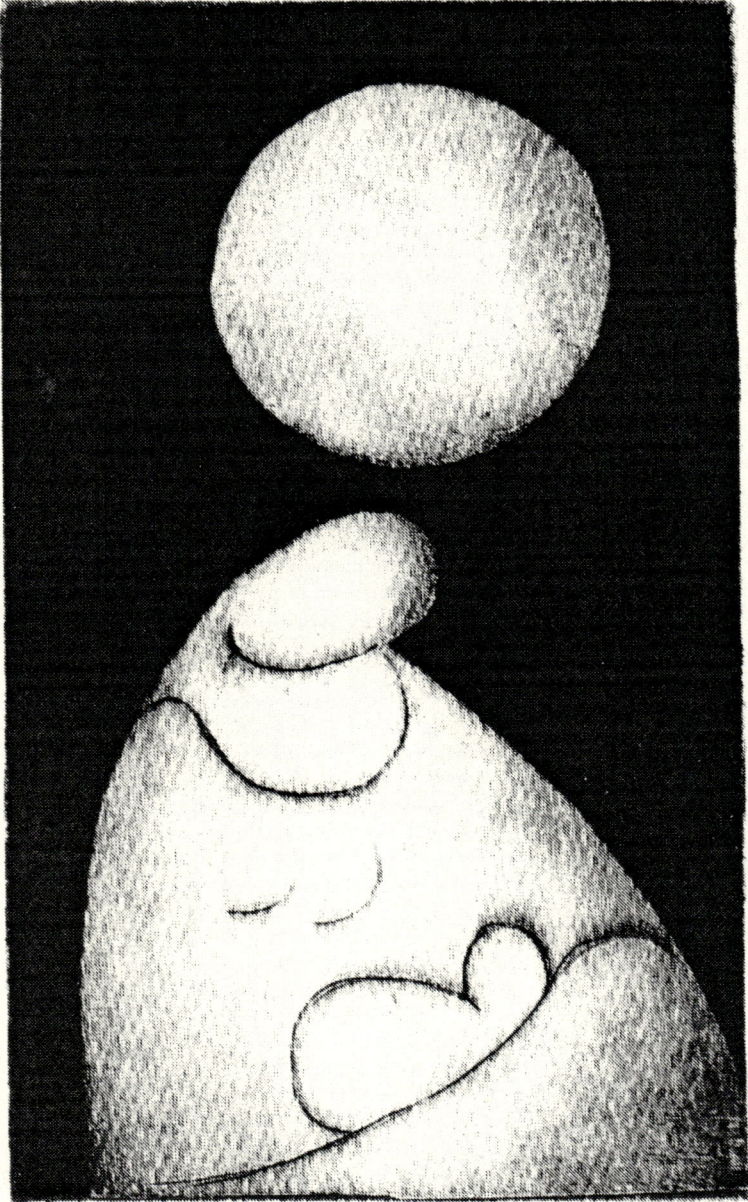

Premie (1)

At 1130pm New Year's Eve, the hour when
good Scots are soused in *Hogmanay,* premie[1] twins
drop effortless into the world; all effort spent in
holding them back ten weeks more.

A dour Gorbals maid of fourteen winters, she speaks
the auld Glaswegian, still an alien tongue to me:
weel ya luk a tha bairn's[2] *fuit*[3]*...tha een*[4]*...*
och they're grutten[5]*...dinna fash*[6] *thissen*[7]*...*

Understands me no better, but has done the job of
popping out these two-pounders as to the
manner born. Although well before the time of
full-court resuscitation—of 28-week 700-grammers

starting life on vents[8] and hyperal[9]—these two know
no rules bar their own, thrive first on neglect—none
foreseeing them celebrating this new year, let alone
later ones—then on dribs of maternal milk, supplement.

She names them for me and my dad (a Galloway man),
at six weeks takes them home to her gran's single-end[10],
could still tuck both in her purse, sling them on one
skimpy shoulder, bonny tough lassie of Scotland the brave.

[1]*premature babies;*
[2]*babe;*[3]*feet;* [4]*eyes;* [5] *crying;* [6]*bother;* [7]*yourselves;*
[8]*artificial ventilation;* [9]*intravenous nutrition (hyperalimentation)*
[10]*one room flat in a high-rise tenement*

Premie (2)

After a day's acquaintance,
Arthur the senior on our rotation
quizzes Esther the Cuban intern:
Were you a premie?

He plans a career in Neonatology,
perhaps has noticed her dolicocephaly[1].
No, it was her middle name, *Milagra:*
common appellation for miracle babies.

Yes, I was born at 28 weeks,
twenty-five years ago this month;
spent two months in an incubator
in the NICU[2] at Columbia.

Her mother, gravida 3, para 0[3] and pregnant
a fourth time, had insisted of her husband
that they leave their homeland, give this
daughter over to god's will and the pride of

New York's neonatal care, driven by prescience,
as she boarded the twin-engine turbo prop in
Cardenas at twenty-five weeks, that this
was yet another pregnancy that would not carry.

[1] *skull elongated from before back*
(common after premature birth)
[2] *Neonatal Intensive Care Unit*
[3] *three pregnancies with no live births*

Consensus and Consent

Kyle's illness can we think be cured.
But its refractoriness has stacked
the odds against him, saying he's lucky
to see his tenth birthday, his next
he may honor in a more celestial place
(wherever that may be). True, some more
experimental (whatever that may mean)
treatments await our testing.

Yesterday's conference brought us
(two faculty and a fellow, three residents
and three nurses, a social worker and two parents-
an ethics committee *ad hoc*) consensus:
our—and his—best course would be
three weeks' therapy that (the fellow
quoting from this month's literature)
reportedly holds promise.

Kyle, consulted today, and glad to be asked
about testing such *terra incognita*,
and *infirma*, says: *No, I want to stay home.*
So be it. He has, we all concede, reached
the age of consent (whenever that might be).
We feel, all in all, taking everything
under consideration, relief that we've
happened upon a decision.

On The *Ganjiang* Canal

Venice has gondolas, Sujhou concrete barges,
Not having the *yuan* for the wood:
House in the hull, tricycles in the bow.

Stone cottages, sheered-off cliffs, abut
the junk-thick enchanted water:
once, twice, thrice, our engine snarls in

ginkgo leaves, roots, plastic bags; the rudder
catches, knocks on a house demanding entrance.
An old woman washes thin cottons

at her garden edge, cackles. Backyard-
and houseboat-people join. A gang of four
chase us on crimson firecracker banks;

hold the lead, disappear elusive,
pop up like marionettes along miles
of coarse yellow sycamore bridges:

Hello! Hello! Giggle madly at our *Ni Hows!*
Two speedboats, modern Marco Polos,
splash us into Sujhou's Grand Canal.

Waiting

Dominic rests on his airbubble cot,
awaiting life's flight from its earthly beat.
He has wearied of searching the way to exist,
of the tubes that fuse to the bag and the pump,
these faceless monitors of the clock
that count his mortal minutes out.

We caregivers charter our critical route
between a stark place and a brittle rock,
while his body lays open its faltering stock
in freefalling spin from heart to gut,
disgorging its wherewithal and prop
with which we fumble to hold it up.

His father's run missing in the wood
to nurse his gun and suckle his guilt,
while his mother stretches her vigil out
not letting her mind embrace it yet,
beholds in his eye the guttering life
that still will not douse its callow light.

For what does he linger? Till this spark
has no more tinder to keep him lit?
Or the organ-dead conspire to draw
his soul to the dark? Or will he wait
till this woman who bends so close above
can finally offer his spirit up?

Will

I yearn to shout for you, dear ill one,
for the waste of muscle wraps drooped
on the once potent bones of youth;
for the frailty of adolescent fingers
creaking in pale contracture, milk
slopping as they strain to lift the cup.

For your scattered wastes of beard, on
gaunt puffed cheeks on which you've
weaved your obdurate line of razor cuts.
For the torment of surrender to a babe again,
to the mother's hand that bathes
your haggard bristling body.

I want to howl, once wild one, swathed in
your bleak crib whence the catheter dangles:
Why do you rail no more against your closing curfew?

Arthroplasty

Tom's fiftieth birthday gift: a new hip;
two in fact, six months apart.
It's the first, though, that calls up
shades: three years in MASH choppers
over Vietnam, on the wrong end of
bullets and other projectiles, but
never of knives, clamps, drills.

Dreams of losing it: of termination
by amputation, of flubs and *snafus*
botchier than any army's; a reverie of
thirty years' service to children at war
with illness: each *h and p*[1] of each
amputee, stupefied he could be so
terrified, so filled with awe of them.

[1] *h and p:* history and physical exam

Fear

2AM on my phone. A hard hail of
fear hits me, icing the voice.
Twisting to calm her word-rush
she asks me over:
> *Why's he getting worse?*
> *When will his fever break?*
> *Will the seizures come again?*

Pauses...then flint-hard challenges:
> *You're not certain. Don't you know?*
> *What's going on? What is it?*

Her sound has unraveled a flash
of my uncle's angry eyes, fearful shouts
pounding my adolescent energy.

I bend back to her, startled to think:
> *No, I don't know why her 12-year-old,*
> *easy host to transplanted tissue,*
> *has built this fever in him, defying logic.*

I know only to look for it, this root of illness,
reflect her terror's sweep, slip from my own
foreboding, not let my zeal overstretch hope,
while bit-by-bit admit a little hopefulness.

And hear the soothe of my mother's murmuring
in the woken night of a shaded dream. The beat

of my mind slows, retakes its presence here,
hears at last this mother hearing me:

her words loosen, flow deeper:
    It's working, isn't it?
She's listening:
    You know, don't you?
Laughs a little:
    Don't change things.
Supports me:
    Glad we talked: thanks.

Intern

Jake's been up all night: his first time.
Beset already with a peds-floor virus
his body's not met before. Presents
(sneezing shy sneezes into palms)
the five-month-old transfer without
transfer note, baffling referral labs.

And looks delighted: pure
three-year-old look, with a beard;
grabs corn hair hanks, slithers elbow
down table, drapes six-foot-two,
scatters paper mound, pink-pig tie-
Hannah's birthday gift—rumpled, snouts
turning curlier. How stunning he is.

Begot

Conceived early in life: sprightly sperm
meets blushing ovum, one thing leading
to another. Call it *psychoneuroimmunology:*
going to the party with dad and
coming home with mom.

Two unicellular gametes
(X and Y let's call them)
toting up to one bicellular zygote:
yours true and glad to be here.

During the *blitzkrieg* it was: May 41,
Spitfire vs *Messerschmitt*, quite a game of
cricket over those two heads
cuddled in bed in the upstairs-front:
23 Park Avenue, Golders Green, NW3,

two gossamer twists entwining their DNA,
as I set out on my sleep of replication,
to dream *Rappunzel* dreams,
to flip *de temps en temps*

the odd somersault like some premature
astronaut, to tune into news from the front.
Not good at first: Pearl Harbor, Bulgarian,
Russian occupations, Rommel at Tripoli,
gas 12 cents per, a new car up to

850 bucks. Getting better: Roosevelt back
for his third term, General Doolittle's
B-17's over Tokyo, Dumbo opening in
New York, Joe Louis ko-ing Buddy Baer.

While I fattened over Xmas,
popped out to three-sisterly applause
late February 42, four weeks behind
Mohammed Ali and four ahead of
Aretha Franklin: a twenty-five-trillion-cell

blueprint all present and correct, until
my foreskin-trimming on the kitchen table.
I've perked up since, had my own share
of *psychoneuroimmuno*-whatever.

Spark

Germ to bud to blossom:
slow dreamer in uterine cocoon;
the lunge of primal quest,
quickening, straining to birth.

Glee in charge: zesty natal
batteries fresh and versatile,
deftly tapping instinct's stores,
sampling each faculty.

Rehearsing senses:
sight and smell and touch and taste;
gum-grip, tongue-curl, lip-pucker,
breath and swallow syncopated.

Planted erect: sturdy trunk in
effortless swoop; dangling on
upside-down stanchion,
face chuckling back.

Circumcision

Day Zero:
upon which you decide against
a surgical career.

He stands scrubbed and
poised aloft for the incision.
His operating suite?
Our kitchen table, 1920's oak,
creaking tractably on its beams.
Your anesthetic? Ah no: babies,
boy ones anyway, have not yet
the nerve to feel the knife.

His audience: Jenny the midwife?
Ah yes: so impressionable to his
prowess. Parker the gardener?
Perhaps: to field the swabs.
Your sisters? Another possible:
such a fine way to learn
male anatomy. Does your foreskin
feel detachment? Do sucklings squeal?

Father maintains *sangfroid,*
bows to Jenny to wipe beads
from the great brow.

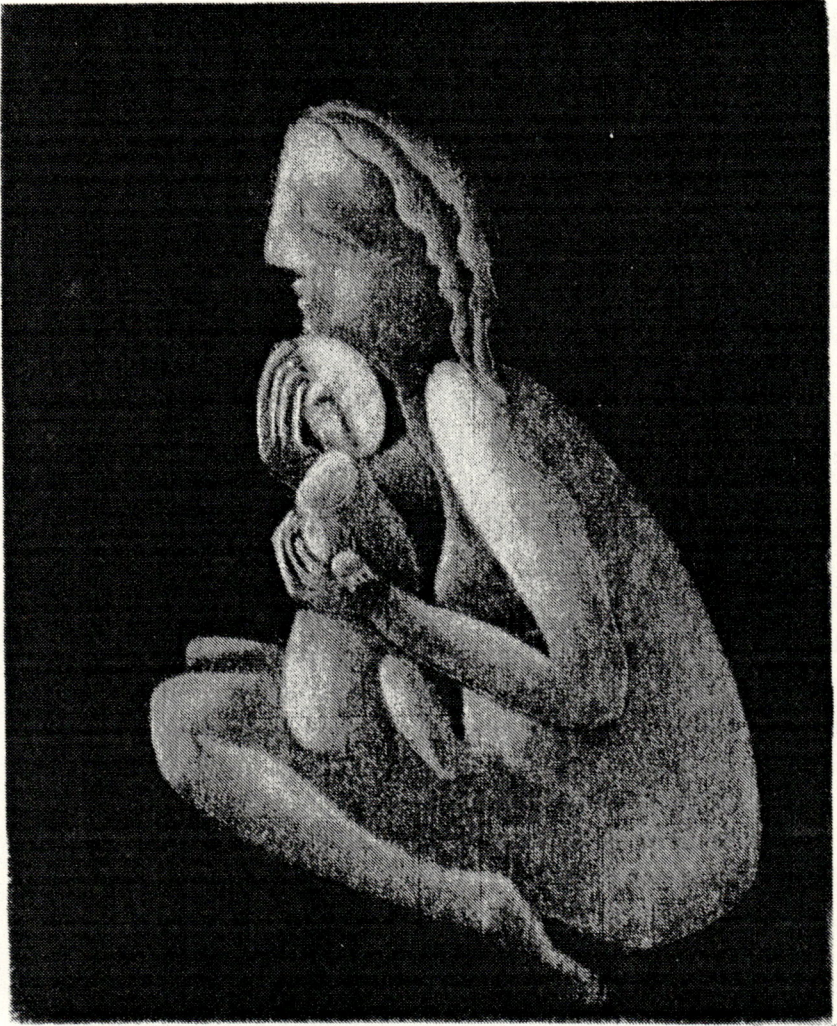

Breakfast

It was such a damp Somerset morning
that she mounded oatmeal into a
Blitz-evacuated bowl, and I sculpted
with my bent and tarnished spoon
deep pools to catch the fall of milk
thinned by the cream-sucking pecks
of fat and thirsty sparrows through
aluminum bottle caps on our kitchen stoop;

watched it tumble down crevasses from tall
grey porridge peaks, furrowed by Lyle's
molten golden treacle lava path
down into glutinous lakes. I would slice
at the cooling edge that held my castle
up, slowly blanketing my stomach
with invader-checking glow before
leaf-kicking conker[1] hunt to school.

[1] English schoolboy slang for horse chestnut

Sex

They were older, shadowy, rich in
feminine mystery; differing in ways
it was aching years until he would articulate.
The big ones were to all the world grown-ups,
while the other, the other *little one*,
was at least for a few precious years
a playmate, with whom he could take
the same baths, snuggle beneath sheets
or within the laundry cupboard's heat
during games of *Sardines*[1], a mentor
for holiday mud pies by Devon streams.

With puberty she too stood off;
so he withdrew to his own boys' gang
as she whispered in doorways and
distant corridors with girlfriends,
beset too by the world of difference.

[1]*An English version of hide-and-go-seek*

Leaving Mother

We slipped, trampled, tripped
on oak roots and knots, poked
through a mat of burned-brown
pine thorn and rotting conker,
autumn damp in August; we little ones
casting away the littler ones that
flew at us, as if casting off spells
that would lay orphanhood upon us.

Over us, arms arced in safety, a canopy
of chestnut, elm, beach, mulberry,
safe haven for solitary travelers: no tigers
nor bears, nor signposts either; before we
moved ahead oblivious, hoisted her
four limbs between us, swung her with the
abandon of children whose mother would
never commit the treason of abandonment;

as she hid her knowing pain in
chuckles, as her cheap print skirt
rucked up, flashing on my 12-year-old sight
astounding golden cami-knickers;
then, tiring, stopped to rest while we
rushed on upon the stolen steps
of night thieves creeping away through
the shades of the dying afternoon.

Children's Doctor

I began by aligning bowed bones;
learned the trick from a Casualty[1] nurse
who lacked the license but took license anyway,
there being no other mentor.

A vain and sloppy art it was:
their pliant ulnas lined up straight whatever I did.
So I learned another skill: cartooning stiffening casts,
my clumsy craft surmounting puckers and whimpers.

Later we'd play, as I chased them
over and under cribs for *H-and-P's*[2]:
outrageously fit-to-bust, go-for-broke,
sweet-as-nut playful they were.

So where do they go to, these young ones?
And where do grown-ups come from?

[1] *English equivalent of ER*
[2] *History-taking and physical examinations*

Class

In their tenth year they journeyed north,
London to Glasgow: Home Counties
to Western isles, keeping their middle-class
mouths shut. Adopted their babies of
Scottish-Irish Glaswegian shipyard folk,
born at Rotten Row Maternity in the sump
of the Gorbals, Europe's thickest slum.

Their parents had saved for their lessons
in elocution, to give them toe-holds on
the upper-middle class, like most of
the *Sassenachs*[1] they met there, mindful
of their own parents before them, who
each took double-barreled surnames
to validate family respectability.

Back in London, they found their veneer
slipped. Beneath their BBC accents
they craved their roots in the lands of
the Celts: his father's Galloway hearth,
his mother's in Cwmbran, hers risen
out of the Rhondda coal valleys, become
better than they might have been.

[1] *English travelers to Scotland*

Immigrant

A downtown Cleveland winter:
sidewalk snow to my knee, a slushy slipstream
on the street. Standing in the freeze line
for the bus, alien sights and sounds assail me,
the numbness skirring about my head,
inklings of terror urgently swept into the mist.

In my office's skimpy solitude I cry until dry,
pain rearing to a new richness, plead for the distant
Matins bell, for steel nibs dipped in blackened
inkwells, for steel mills dipped in dust, for beer-swilling
rugger-boys downing ten pints without a pee,
for embankment nights of cold hands on
warm breasts, for the snap and glisten of
what else was there for a hearty boy to know.

Woman (1)

Five feet, fifty kilo,
she hoists me easily
onto her back's keel.

I draw in her sweat,
fresh as lilies, stretch
on her taut strut.

Rock, slip, brace, heft,
await my turn to tote
her light might.

Woman (2)

Her lids drop to the delicate rubbing
of index and thumb pulp on her
red and black pens; trading them back
and forth, back and forth, secreted in
the folds of her chart. Her eyes are
dressed in a hot rose coat resonant
of summer's fervor and shadow. Silent

but for the steady click, click, of those ends
in their up-down rhythm on the breast
of her scrubs, below the four-point pin
decked with amber and emerald stone.
The fingers voluptuously flex and ease,
flex and ease, as she rests her wrist's weight
on her thigh, lips pouted in thought.

Woman (3)

The red letters on black,
jiggling on the mound of her tee
as she breasts the tide of
Hartsfield's wayfarers,
announce: *'Atlanta Bra...'*,
the *'...ves'* concealed by
a pleasing ruck of fabric.

Check-In

Eyes mouths cheeks chins tuck
down and in, weight upon inert fists,
not looking out at the company.
Covert gazes fix on checklists fanned
across this silent table outside
the children's cancer ward.

At its top, Tom tallies each clinic visit,
each child, even the infants, tagged
with last name and disease; then
startles us, scandalously, with jokes that
prompt a scattershot of first eye contact.

The shift to the ward census lures
more vigilance: names tied closer
to pathos, pain, foreboding. Frowns,
quickly caught, supplant the glaze,
as we sense it settle a little, this
wary thaw toward the week's work.

Health Care

When Jake bleeds into his lungs I realize
(though I've known him and his mother and
his brain tumor and his chemo and his veins
too long) I don't know them well enough
to ask: *How hard d'you want us to try here?*

Four am and Jake's refusing O_2, let alone
the ET[1] tube. His BP's as high as his
blood count is low. He's spluttering: *Let me
f...ing die!* And *I'm not your f...ing sweetheart!*
Yelling at me between bloody coughs.

Too right, you're not. So how come I'm using
such language of endearment with this
thirteen-year-old monster who, from the look
of him and his mother, never knew what it was
to be held, let alone hugged, in his life.

The room's choked with people, machines, clutter,
the floor awash: used and dropped syringes,
leaking plastic saline bags, blood from his lungs,
veins, arteries, paper (pencilled records of orders
bellowed, lab readings, torn-off EKG[2] strips).

His mother won't leave his left side,
curses us, and him, with a stream of
f...ing a...h...s. While we struggle, sliding and

slipping, to get mask in place, arms strapped,
four of us to hold down the flailing feet.

Meanwhile, back in the nurses' changing room
(unlocked at this hour: we pinned down
the time later), someone else is at work:
lifting credit cards, a checkbook, fifty dollars
from a student's wallet: a good haul.

[1] *Endotrachael tube*
[2] *Electrocardiogram*

Ruby Red

Her body fragrant from alveolar showers,
floats forth our curvy spheroid Ruby red;
her cheeks aglow with O_2s heartening powers
she charts her course for that far capillary bed.
The rosy roller rides the aortic road,
unmindful of her distant splenic fate,
through arteriolar backwoods bears her load-
the wastrel CO_2 recoils too late.
But macrocytic changes lie ahead,
and days of crenation speedily ensue;
she's targeted for pyknosis, so 'tis said;
our once pink heroine fades a waning blue.
And so poor Ruby meets her final test,
in gentle hemolysis rolled to rest.

Ode to Lou and Will

I tell you the tale of two fine friends of mine
named *Louis Leuk* and his buddy *Willy White*
who never miss a chance to wine and dine
on parasites who venture out at night;
old Will and Lou can squeeze through any crack
to phagocytose E coli's by the bunch;
for they love a really buggy kind of snack
and streptococci make a perfect lunch;

they'll catch them napping in their mouldrin' layers
for they are a sniffin' snatchin' kind of men,
and microbes kneel to say their rotting prayers
before them as they chemotax their den.
Let us to Will and Louis proffer praise
and love them for their antimicrobial ways.

Signs

Eddie's body bewilders them:
pocked at birth with livid leukemia lumps.
People eye them through eleven in-out-
hospital months. When the pneumonia hits,
we say: *A mercy.* Sam, he's seen enough,
but Rose: *No! You'll be wrong again.*

She has her way. Sticking the tube down
takes more brute force than *forte,*
as he gasps and grasps at life.
We hang on four days, settings stable,
then gather—caregivers, Sam, their folk,
say: *It's wrong—he can't live.*

But Rose: *No! I need a sign.* There
we stick, Sam yielding, loving her.
We understand, can't be where you are.
No one's right or wrong.
We'll wait on the sign.
And go about our weekends.

Thirty minutes later, a page in Publix
grocery aisle: *Tube's out, can't get*
it back, blood, bedlam, can you get here?
By then they've done it.
Rose, watching them mop up,
clings, moans: *Stop! It's the sign.*

We wait on their kin, traffic bad,
a home game on, write our charts:
We've talked it through, parents agree,
are ready. Don't prolong it (first do
no harm). We go over *how.* Sam cradles
Eddie's body, Rose's sister Sam's.

Rose flees. We fill Eddie's body and mind
with *fentanyl.* Extubate. A gasp. Darkening.
We hear his heart a minute. Then *not.*
Rose sweeps in, clasps him, keens on and on.
Their folk: *Can't we give her something?*
Let's wait see, she needs to do it.

Twenty-five minutes pass. She calms,
welcomes us, invites us to hold him,
say *goodbye.* Taking our cue we
cry too, laugh a bit, feel the ease,
hold each other, think on Eddie's life
and his good death.

Protective Isolation

(I remember every patient who's occupied that room:
—ICU nurse)

These sterile layers of air
encase her, tenuous as thoughts
that spark poems. On this parchment
she pens an epiphany,
to lay a cloth of flesh
upon her sanctum's barrenness.

Her muse: have her predecessors
healed and borne off their
mortal burden? Or does their
presence still share in this
meager space with her, hosts and
guests, a lingering assembly

of ghosts that take their
turn unraveling the drama
of this poem she lives?
Can then her muse reform these
shadows, fragments of the
universal mind, to substance?

She feels these shades curled
with her about her pillows, lifting
the pain, easing it around the
edge of this cool draft, blowing it
clear with the motes that
swirl away beneath her door.

Cell Shed

I lean in among
the plastic tubes besetting you,
my breath voluntary,
yours urged.

Our cells mingle each with
the other's, spilling in spindrift
of air-water-ice
between mouths.

You, going, dying,
take my life to rest.
I, living, left, draw in,
exhale your seed.

You Gotta Laugh

It is never too late to be who you might have been

George Eliot

Clayton's earned a poem: he and his stock of outrageous jokes:
Gotta get your priorities right—right?

To my grown-up gravity, telling him he's one 16-year-old
whose cancer's a doubtful starter for departing his body
ahead of his soul, he bounces back with the one-liner
sprung from his MC genius, intro-ing the keynoter for
last week's RC retreat that he'd taken a year to plan,
that shortchanged him on time for illness and other trivia:
If you weren't who you are you could be him, or me!

All bets are off on this one: I'm swimming less in
the mainstream with the old trouts of prognosis, more in
the sunny shallows where the minnows of miracle play:
Predictions don't slow me down any.

Prancing and dancing, smokin' and jokin', taking his bow
and his exit down our Cancer Center corridor out of
Chemo-world to check out other prospects...

Journeys and Sojourns

This past eighty days I've journeyed busily,
while Dana's fourteen-year-old body's stayed in place.
Not from her choice. I've hastened to appointments,
gone home nights, often to the mall and through the park,
strolling my yard, biking my neighborhood,
while she made mind-jumps home across the line.

I saw the arch once in St. Louis, leaf-fall in Atlanta;
she for Halloween made it to her window,
but mostly from bed to chair and back,
as best her softened muscles would concede.

I've been to *Bennigans,* driven through *MacDonalds*
while she checked in some fancy fantasy place:
a table laid with wieners, apple sauce and *Yo-Yo,*
recent visions of turkey, sweet potatoes.

I caught movies, once the *Mac Attack*;
she gazed down the hanging TV hours,
sharp mind glazed with inactivity.
Each day's visit I'd bring joyful mouthfuls
of life's new happenings, but her buds are blunt;
right now she finds it hard to taste the fun.

Asclepius

Socrates, latter-day peripatetic philosopher,
stands from 11 to 9 outside St Elizabeth's
Greek Orthodox blowing his clarinet into
the free air of America, storing the *drachmai*
to bear him home to lie by his wife beneath
Attic soil; echo of Asclepius' Delphic temples,
half a world and three millennia away,
where Ulysses was healed with ballads
more than bandages, where Pythagoras
sang daily for catharsis to fortify his humors;

Asclepius, to whom mother Athena gifted
two phials of Gorgon blood, one to heal,
one to kill, whom the Greeks made father
of physicians, whom Zeus smote with thunder
for learning too well how to raise the dead;
banishing his father Apollo to herd
Thessalian ewes, who became patron of
the Muses by trading a shepherd's pipe
for Mercury's lyre, tossing his caduceus into
the bargain, about which were entwined
two serpents;

                    not to be confused, as did
our 16th century physician forebears,
with Asclepius' own single-snaked caduceus
gracing his temples over the Bay of Corinth,
where the priests beguiled the sick with

dreams and dramas, chants and images,
where the *Orpheotelestai* danced the
movement of the stars in spheres about them,
where the underworld of spirits came forth to
bless the sick until they rose up from their beds.

No wonder Socrates goes home in his mind to die.

East and West

I eye three hundred Asians:
columns of forty, rows of eight,
cruisers on China Eastern's
triple MD-11 turbofans,
heading north west at 4.20AM US
east coast time from Seattle over
Kodiak Island and the Arctic cap,
11,000 kilometers across
the dateline into the Far East;

and see each face is different,
like I'd always suspected:
faces of Far Easterners,
more like us Westerners
from back East going West
with them than different.

They have no difficulty seeing
their difference, only seeing
ours. A Vietnamese woman
tells me she can't sort Japanese
from Chinese faces, but their
body language betrays them.

Brittle-eyed, I eye this
cumulative facial miracle:
99% the same, 1% composing
such ineffable uniqueness
as to distinguish each from each
without thought.

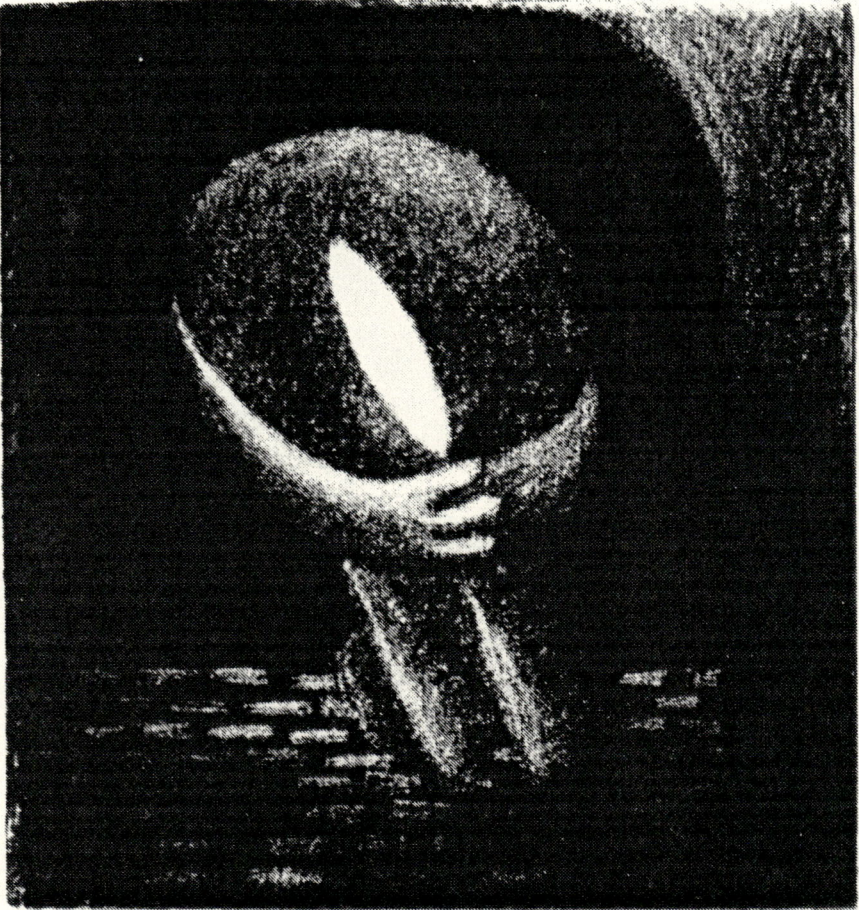

Requiem

Illness, to us caregivers, seems
a faulty way to problem-solve.
But faced with terminality
you felt relief, had earned
at last an honorable discharge
from a losing side, from a
no-stake no-aim no-win game.
To pinpoint why you were here
seemed moot to you, old life-leaver.

You cloaked, from shame, joy at
release from requisite struggle,
feigned a brave face, dissembled
your compliance with our pills
(care's conspiracy given and taken),
scraped from us a last laurel for a life
sidelined in numb neglect, foretasted
death day as birthday, doused all
your years' candles in a last blow.

Victorian Scene

Teatro Colon: curtain down
on *La Nozze di Figaro.* We
stretch from our gallery box's
velvet-padded chairs,
down the marble staircase
beneath the chandeliers' faded
gilt, out to curbside limos:
midnight on *Corrientes.*
At the light, from below the
awnings of *La Confiteria Ideal*
(home to high tea for English
emigres) steps

another original:
eyes of bottomless black, hair
lit with firelight, skirt raveled
at the hem. Ten or eleven by the
breast buds, but under height,
with jutting ribs. *A dollar, Signor?*
She offers one deft lewd gesture,
this proud *portenia*[1], to Edgar
stretching to wind our window
against the saintly face.

We sit quiet in the heat at the light.

[1]*Portenia: Woman of the port (of Buenes Aires)*

Beijing Clean-Up

Her small one squats in uncurbed glee
on the *Guanghua* sidewalk, awaits the paper
she's fetching from her tricycle at the curb
by the pepper and peanut gunny sacks
spilt in tall piles on pristine sheets.

Like an acrobat she twirls him face down
on her lap, to wipe through the gaped triangle
in his cut-out pantaloons, then wrap the matter
in the *China Daily News*.
                         They pass on
unheeded together, he perched in the carrier
up front, she at her pedals, weaving with
seven million others along the spotless street.

Last Rites

Sunday morning: in the drive-through
outside the Emergency Room idle
four red and white county ambulances
that double as fire trucks, engines puttering
their impromptu four-part harmony.

Mr Mackie, erstwhile Hurricanes linebacker,
squats in the ER doorway, hiding from the heat,
scrunches the frail plastic bag that holds
his three-year-old daughter's underwear,
embroidered with Peter Rabbit motifs.

Soon he'll head home, lift them from their bag,
stand over his sink, wash the blood from them.
The ambulance driver joins his mate; they start
to sluice down the flooring with their hoses.
After the vomit and blood the water runs clear.

Risks

Holding this mother, who has just hurled her
body upon me over the PICU crib that enfolds him,
to sob as I squeeze a white-coat-pocket's-worth
of grubby Kleenex between us,

I flinch across her shoulder at his nurse,
at the savor of Marlboro Lites, entertain
between shallow breaths irrelevant,
irreverent hazards-of-health-care thoughts,

guide us in a slow one toward two corridored rockers
(gifted last month by the family of Anna Cathryn,
god rest her) amid the coming-and-going
train-on-a-track voices:

That premie in Pod 2...
Let's go see the babies—not the ICU ones...
She matched at Brown and OSU...
You want I bring you a sub up?

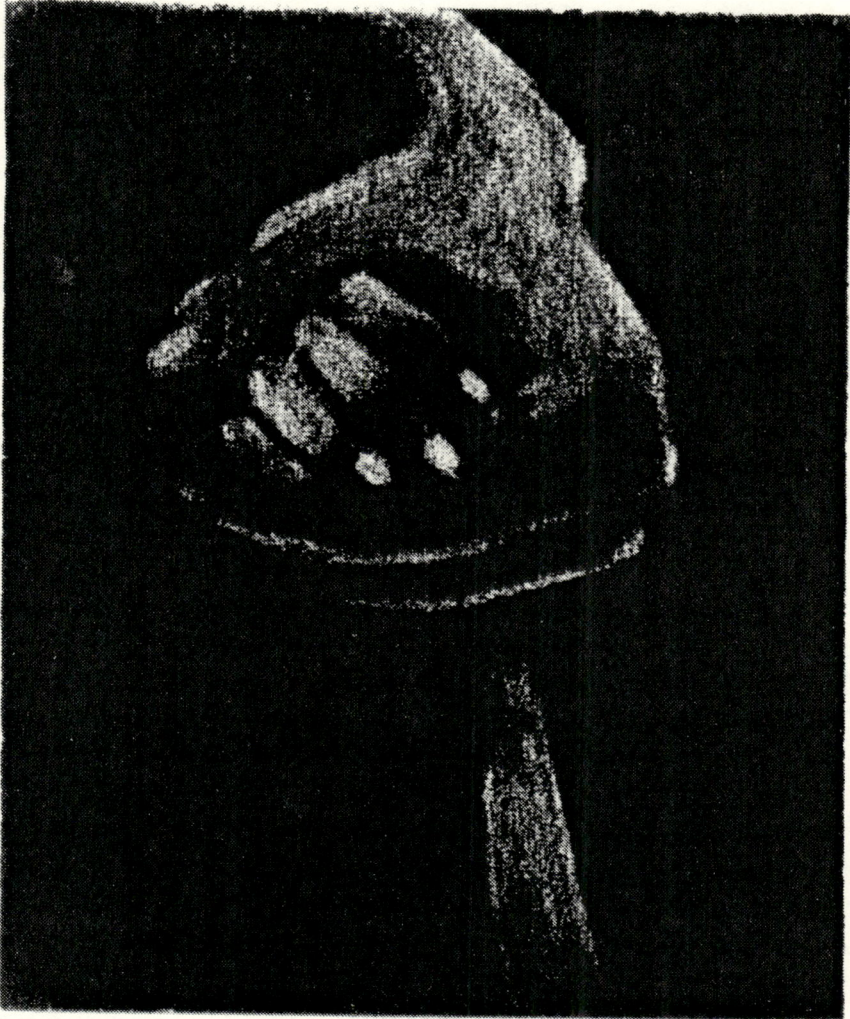

Cat and Crow

The crows glide over Archer, between palms and holm oaks,
over cars speeding from the 13th Street light to the strip mall at 34th.
Last week a children's dentist left his clinic in the dusk
after bidding goodnight to his students, to be slapped from
his bike, brought in dead to the ER three minutes away:
fatality number fifty of the decade of the Magic Mile.
They've not figured how to slow things down.
                                        At palm-top level,
five stories above the crows, you sit on the bed to tell this father
his son's story, repeat your words so you can hear them too. Knowing
no way around it you'd jumped in, unknowing if they could hear you
or not, with words you're unused to, fresh from your fellowship,
shielded by your seniors until now from shedding such tidings.

As the crows swoop on the traffic, the boy asks: *Can my cat visit?*

Elegy

You're newly dead, *sans* wig,
seventeen-year-old virgin whom
I'd loved. Your face is almond wax,
preamble to gelling and decay.

Your mother clasps my hand as I
kiss your bald head. She has been
engrossed with the new baby,
you with beating the odds: the

isolation of illness estranging you,
although cancer is family business.
At first, learning it had recurred,
you were steadfast: *No more chemo.*

But, sensing the creeping loss of
bladder and legs, bit-by-bit
you'd come around, readied yourself
for ablation, for the chance at life.

As the fight ignited you'd stayed
wigged and cool, mind set.
Until it ended, and you'd said
goodbye to me. You had spoken

little to me before, but they told me
you liked my silences, trusted me,
my faith there was some purpose
to this wasted resource of a life.

Lovers

We absent ourselves at the buffet.

And they, unchaperoned, curl themselves
around their starched white-linen table-corner.
She giggles at his nose bumping the arc
of lemon peel atop the glass, chatters,
entranced by his absorption, drubs her
eager sandalled heels upon the chair-bar.
He gleams, rapt in her solemn womanly wit,
a callow swain again, a murmurer of compliments,
leans in until their foreheads touch and rub:

grandfather, granddaughter, under their veil of covert talk.

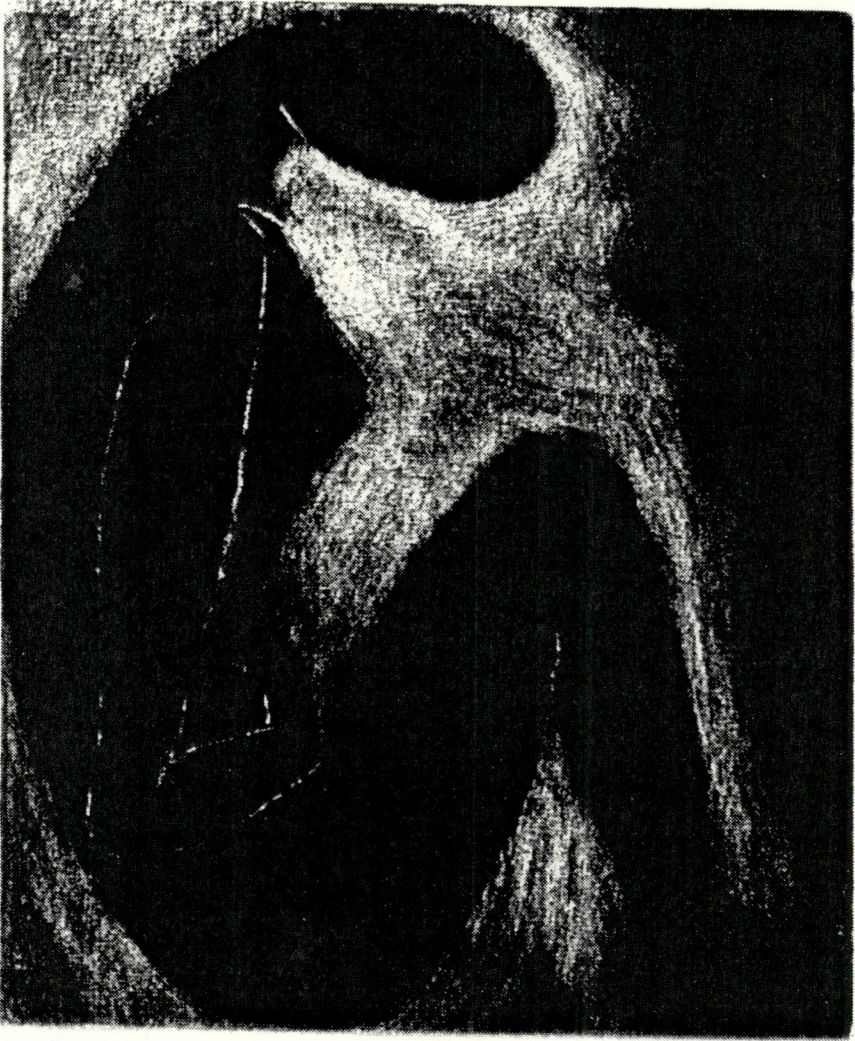

Chorale

Death in Intensive Care's no easy thing
to orchestrate: we're pro-life whose
raison d'etre is trainwreck-resurrection[1].
Dan, though, you conduct your own: compose
your hospice passion behind the pod-2 curtain,
as your soloists nonplus us with their readiness:
Tony, biker-dad in teenage threads, mother Moe
raging that we're so loath to let you *do it.*

Meanwhile you rehearse us in your *Requiem.*
First the prelude from your gurney: *In two hours I'm going.*
Tony returns: *Fine, son, go for it.*
Two hours later you seize; lungs, liver, kidneys
shut down, no cause we can see. So our tubes must
chant their antiphony of sampling, testing, purging,
as your ventilator's coda stays your exodus. Hoarse,
helpless, you rasp at last: *S..., let me home. Home.*

At last we hear you, *maestro,* attune ourselves
to listen, stop our lab-draws, blink out our lights.
Moe murmurs: *Thank you.*
Celestial chords wash your pod, nurses echoing angels.
You rest, tone your simple needs: *some ice, a popsicle.*
Tony and Moe blend arias: Gulf-fishing-days lying out,
bald behind shades, building a tan and girl appeal;
one school day 300 you hardly knew partied with you.

Tony intones of you in the past tense: *Dan was a fixer,*
he'd have fixed this if he could. Had a multicolored wig

for chemo days for the young ones (one little black one
shared his bed). But he'd stay not a needless minute,
up-chucked all the way home while I fed the baby.

Moe: *We're having him cremated. Tony, he'll spread his*
on that Pennsylvania field where he made his first goal.
Me, I'll scatter mine on the Gulf where he hooked his fish.

[1] *Resuscitating badly injured people*

September 11

We light our candles,
embark on a million
silent moments.

This is what we have;
this, and the potency
of tears bled like wounds

laid open on this rock,
our Mother, letting
the universe shine through.

Astounding grace,
show us new ways
to imagine.

Dying

Time
to let your life out for a billow:
to gust your antic rainbow kite at death,
making it less drab, less bland, less dead;

time
to dose yourself a physic of mirth,
mania, momentousness, my dear one;

time
to leave the work of living for the play of dying;

time
to turn handstands into your closing with it,
to bounce on it with bow and curtsy, clasp
its hands in yours, swirl it into the *sarabande,*

so your play may end in merrily ever after:
comedy's as vital a thing as tragedy.

Phase II Trial[1]

A lifetime of steady schooling-
alphabet-rote, number-recital,
history date, geography location,
shoe-tie, jump-rope, bike-ride, slow-dance,
how we are born, grow, age, die-
hasn't readied you for the cold synopsis
of our Consent Form.

A lifetime of educated modesty-
bedroom door closing, body covering,
segregating girls from boys,
separate amenities for men and women,
learned euphemisms for your body's functions-
hasn't readied you for our free inspection
of your daily *portapotti.*

A lifetime of practicing precaution-
sheltering from harm, not overtaxing,
running in the middle of the pack,
getting by with least amount of effort,
okay grades without distinction-
hasn't readied you for the chill reality
of this life-challenge.

A lifetime of careless risk-taking-
climbing oak trees, diving rock pools,
home runs, hardballs, headlocks, hook shots,
driving dragsters, shooting the tube,

rash roller-coaster thrill-seeking-
hasn't readied you for our accolades
for this your hero's role.

[1] *Experimental cancer therapy*

Twins

At thirteen, Eve's outgrown her mother,
who still in her dreams hears my tread
down the Cancer Center corridor,
my pause beside each exam room door
as she awaits the verdict of the count.

I want to tell her: *Rea, bathe your sadness*
in almond oil, wash your feet in cool water,
breathe through your left nostril twenty times
before sleep. But I'm shy with such
six-thousand-year-old advice.

Eve's here to quiz me: a school project.
Why did you become a doctor? We sit in rockers
facing each other in 94B's nurses' station.
She tosses her questions fearlessly, her mother
silent. *Why a pediatrician? An oncologist?*

Does she remember? I loop my own back at her:
Do you remember me? The hospital? The nurses?
All those shots? Do you remember Ana your sister?
Yes, she says to each, this serious survivor:
Yes, I remember Ana my twin we left here.

One question unasked, unanswered: *Why was*
that one taken, while you remain to question me?

Bone Marrow Tale

One shouldn't in December 91 die
of sepsis. Michelle did; watching
it come she asked your pardon,
Dr Anne, her voice centered
between laughter and whimper:
sorry I kept you up all night.

You answered, woman to woman, hey
that's okay, laughed, cried,
kept up with your business
of helping her live, or die,
seeing no contradiction between
loving care and capability.

With transplanted leucocytes laid low
(God's gift in limbo) she grew
a germ in her blood, an ulcer
along tender shy mucosa: meeting,
they made merry in unholy marriage
within her. Raw rectum, virgin labium

debauched by wounds not even love's
genius could restore: taut skin
blotched by blue and purple billow,
never a splash of healthy yellow.
You grappled to insert the Foley, count
the dropping urine as her kidneys failed.

Supine, naked she lay, 18 years'
maiden modesty relinquished
to cold comfort (flimsy sheet too
weighty); complain? No murmur.
Weary, shocked as she, you eyed
the demarcation line's advance

tracking up belly, down thigh,
the pride of late-20th-century
antibiotics faltering in its path.
And now, with deepest sadness,
as she moaned through coma's clasp
of mercy, you tuned the morphine up.

Afterwards you cuddled sister Kirstin,
asked about her horse, confided:
between you and me I'm real scared
of horses; prompting my thought:
not much frightens you, proficient
lover of hurting humans.

I doff cap and mask and booties
to you: lucky Michelle to draw your
weekend call. Your toughness bore you
through cold report to Monday-morning
quarterbacks, as the scene replayed
and lightly freed your tears.

Not a germ's nor a transplant's tale,
but of partners in illness who loved well.

Joy

Five AM: they call me through July-night-end rain
to head-pounding pulse-falling Dan, of the
platelets long dead, and no Asian donor in town
better than a *C-match*[1] save sister Joy, of the
six-year-old veins too frail for sixteen-gauges.

And his last knowing act, as blood floods his
ventricles on CAT scan and the seizures begin,
is to sing solace to mom, dad, nurse, me,
Joy and himself, into the rising dawn. Joy
watches the stifling of maternal sobs

(woman of Xian, inured against public sorrow)
but, unschooled in this, cries her own holy water,
while clutching mom's hand for last rites,
while painting my portrait in the passage,
while breakfasting on scrambled egg, choco-milk,

while asking in her thrush's voice:
Why must my brother die? Is he an angel yet?
Are you my friend now? So Nurse Sonnie asks:
Do you want to say goodbye? She: *Can I hear him*
with the stethoscope? But her daddy grasps her,

bears her back, nor do these parents touch their
fading son farewell, for fear they trap his soul
in our world. Instead, she says goodbye to me,

paint from her portrait sticky on the pulp of
each finger as the elevator shuts between us.

¹Matching for blood donor compatibility

Gottlieb's Pride

At the east end of the mansion front
that abuts Fort Lauderdale's grand canal,
a garage that could house five Camry's.
Within glimmers the sleek white-on-beige
of the Rolls Royce coupe; beside it the pride
of German internal combustion,
the coal-black Daimler of similar vintage.

She chooses the latter, proffers me
the passenger seat. I slide my hand down
the mahogany, sink into the redolent leather,
drop into a dream:

                    seven years old,
perched beside Uncle Ron the magistrate
in his 1949 Daimler roadster, coasting over
the hilly highways of South Wales, the needle
under his gentle press rolling effortless
toward the hundred mark.

                    Cars were scarcity
to me, one time a passenger in Mr Ledbury's
Ford Popular, perhaps twice in Uncle Ken's
Hillman Minx; Ron's Welsh jaunt lasted
in memory like the magic gulps of my first
nectarine in Great Aunt Jessie's August garden.

My mind lurches back to Fort Lauderdale,
to I-95's fast lane bound for Miami
at a jerky fifty. Behind us chains of cars
swing out to our right, swerve close by
my window, back onto the fast lane.

I look anywhere but at them, tune into
my driver's voice raised over that of
her skittery friend cringing behind.
She jerks down once more to forty, curses
the speedster swerving back into our lane
a foot beyond our bumper.

                       I spy the towers
of Miami, notice my breath: short, jerky as
our car's. Better to have taken the Rolls.

Clay

For Bill Strickland

The sun floods the honey-brick arches of the
Manchester Craftsmen's Guild. This was how,
at fifteen, hemmed in and loitering, he had stopped
to watch the sunlight of Wednesday afternoon
slant through the window of the decaying
downtown Pittsburgh schoolroom, lighting upon
the man at the wheel who shaped the swirling mold.

This was how he had seen at once how the world
could be, where the light was; had stepped in,
told the man, *I want to learn what that is, learn
what you do.* For fifteen years the man had taught him:
Mold, work the world like clay. So his flock of numberless
children turn the wheel, throw the refractory brick,
pedal and shape and fire and glaze the earth.

Hoi Entomoi

Thank you, my pesty bestiola,
in your grubby cubby-hola,
with legs numbering 4 to 104, or more,
for scouring the crumbs upon my floor
and sweeping clean beneath my door,
tidying *ad infinitum*
each item *reconditum*
shed beneath my big bedspread,
or even about my slumbering head,
for hopping and popping every
yummy crummy into your tummy.

Things are much tidier
since the hairy-scary spidier
gulped up in one big sup
each itsy-witsy bitsy that she spiedier.

So before you thoughtlessly villipend,
or send to its tail-end,
each common or garden slippy slug
or harmless mommy mealy-bug,
so snug beneath your cozy rug,
remember your silver-spotted skipper,
or other gallinipper,
would rather have you leave her
a little bit of litter for her bed-sitter.

I rather surmise their inferior size
has diminished these creatures' station
in the misplaced estimation
of our human civilization;
at least that's my speculation.

So come to tea Mr flea, Mrs bee,
Miss pretty fritillary;
check my larder, friend cicada,
stay a while, master snile,
rest your feet-o, sirrah 'squito,
on the house, little louse,
chug-a-lug, spittle bug,
that's the ticket, granny cricket,
pull up a chair, my long-hair woolly bear.

Our two specioi,
hoi entomoi and hoi anthropoi,
could each other quite enjoy,
I dare soi.

Rive Gauche

A decade ago, through the open window
of my fourth floor room in *le Pension de la Place*,
at the hub of that foreign city of six million,
I heard again the children's cries from the
familiar park, two blocks further south of the river,
raised over the deep old call of trucks and
commuter cars diffusing that late lonely
Monday afternoon. The echoes of their songs
drew me back, to stand shy at the trellised fence,
like a child myself on his first day, until the voice of
that five-year-old lifted itself to me:

J'ai perdu mon chapeau, j'ai perdu mon chapeau!
Then, as I moved quickly to retrieve the hat from
its burial place under the sand, dust it off,
hand it to her: *Vous etes mon ami, Monsieur,*
she responded, standing tall and grave, as if the
park belonged to her, bowing to me. *Ca ne fait rien,*
I answered, more to myself than her, *Ca ne fait rien.*

Breaking News

In the cancer clinic
people brush us as we seek
the sanctuary of an empty room
and visit death together.

Hi: (let me speak
only to sentence-end not,
anxious and artless, beyond
as if longer could delay it);

As my mouth opens
abandon-memories chill me,
and your real and present anger:
(I'll smile, stay light, not dodge;

You deserve that
I look you in the eye):
Karen, dying's fine, I say
(to myself: what do I know?)

As you, knowing death
too well, assuage me;
you fear not dying but
doing it (who wouldn't?) in diapers.

So off you go,
share your final glimmerings out;

your grad-school money
will pay the funeral

save for a last
letting-go-round Disney;
you'll binge too on allotting
your two-decades' treasures

(death like life
being costly: justly so,
two such precious things).
You're shy telling Josh:

I still (presumptuously)
love you; in time you'll
ride, in morphine-trails,
your last carousel.

Eroica

Teenagers die hard.
Their youth and power and beauty
hang so—although they'll never
lead the pack nor graduate.

Their feet *will* still beat to
rap songs and rock songs as
they flail at life, flash,
then dim, like stars—their idols.

And their cavities fill
and their blood counts jump
and their muscles fail
and their culverts stop forever.

Then most fall silent, have
lost the voice to scream:
Why me, why me?
into the waiting air.

But puberty and death don't lie
like lovers together. And here are
some who hang there, some
rebels mutinous, hot and high

on the ramparts. See this one:
grunting her last gasp

behind her lipstick gash
behind her O$_2$ mask,

her painted finger points
entwining flares of light between
her boyfriend's fingers.
And this one—who won't

die, *won't* die: bleeding,
decaying, defying, demanding
one more of our experiments
in renewing vital things.

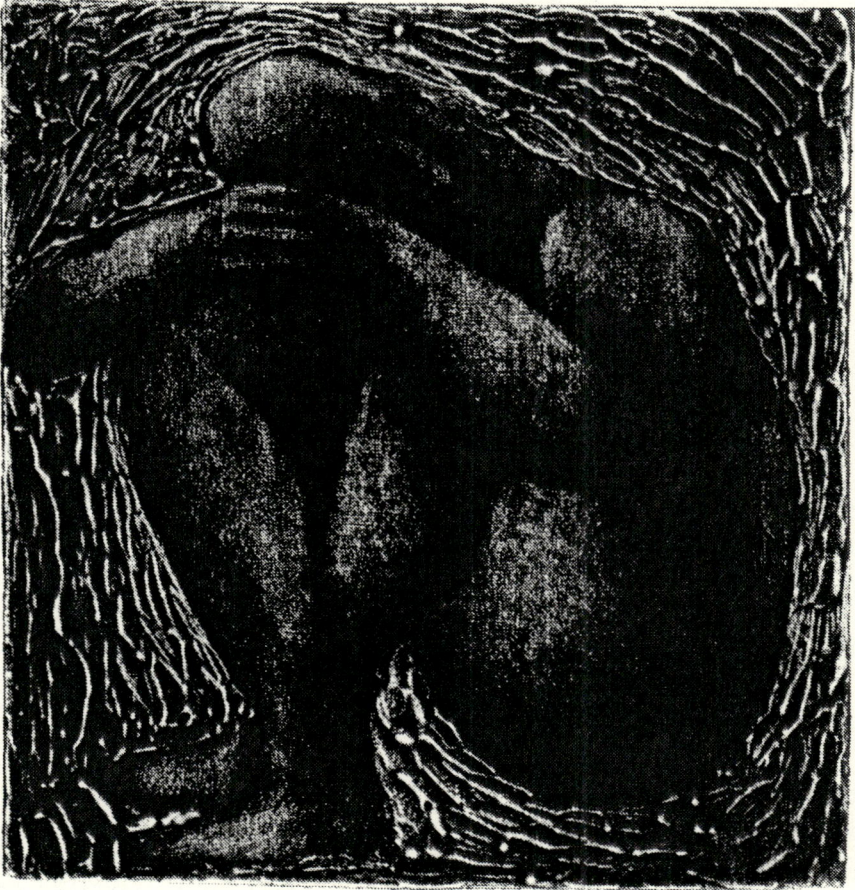

Color of Grief

You press your body toward him,
hiccupping your chair upon the
new laid Cancer Center carpeting.
His bolts reflexive back, into itself.

You talk to him about his body's curfew,
lay upon him his blood's apostasy.
The words arc the deep cold space between
you, fifty, articulate white professor, and

him, fourteen, silent boy of color,
quarantined in separate isolations.
His mother waits outside the fettering
hoop of talk that shackles both of you within.

His eyes slip once in acquiescence,
schooling of black-white deference
in each bright darting quadrant that
never fix their fullness on you.

At last the head droops subjugate
to your words, tongue licking
furtive at the boulder tear rolled
slowly down upon a young man's cheek.

Circles

Afterwards the circles of our talk
snap. The family wraps their own
about them: mother, sister, father, son;
say their private things, their prayer.

While we regroup in our own insider ring:
  Were there other things we
  could have said, should have said,
  about it? Were better left unsaid?

No: they got a hold of it, need only to
smooth answers to the jagged questions:
  Could it take one so young?
  So strong? Of what? Exactly? When?

Our borders are chalk hoops
Scored on the floor. Within, we write our
separate texts of it. Between, the tension
stands: this no talk could break.

Candor

At eight years old, the cancer running rampage,
Joe perches on my office sofa edge
thigh-to-thigh with mom
(who has enjoined me: *Square with him*).

But I beat about the bush a bit,
then come at last to it: Joey:
you're going to die, go to heaven—
words lost in his howl, like a wolf's,

the hurling of his body into
the yellow print dress's recesses.
Three minutes at least of this, this keening,
as we eye each other panicked:

whatever else was right to do this wasn't it.
Then, as instantly, on a long-drawn-in
breath's end, he stops, swivels out, flicks a look,
spots tears on cheeks of mom, dad, nurse, me,

determines he's grieved enough: time to
lighten up, knowing me at other times a joker,
a wearer of odd socks, funny noses. He spies
memos, charts, photocopies, journals,

jetsam of an urgent life, bespattering my carpet,
and becomes the stand-up comic,
offers his own joke: *Didn't your mom
teach you to pick up after yourself?*

Slant

I'd read them the poem about the eight-year-old
I'd told was going to die: his parent's wish, so
there'd be no conspiracy of silence between them.
How he'd howled for three minutes, then stopped
on an in-breath, played the stand-up comic, offered
jokes. The point about truth-telling opening the
sluice gate to emotion, trust-building, those things.

Afterwards two surgeons approached me;
one in judgment, as if to say: *How dare you?*
The other tender: *Sorry, I just couldn't do it.*
Tell the truth but tell it slant. That's me,
my failure perhaps. Surgeons are really softies.

Acknowledged poems compress: *Perhaps you'd*
worked up to it a bit? Yes: I beat about the bush a bit,
but then came at last to it: Joey, you're going to die.
Candor I'd called the piece. Was I *too* candid?
They'd thought so. For me, I knew he knew.
He knew I knew it: straight, no slant in that.

Prospect

You belong here at the world's fire;
don't hang at its edge.
The bad guys are good guys too,
mean well, even as you delve deep
to prize their meaning.

We can lift the rocks off each other,
lick our wounds, be
fathered, mothered, set upon each other's knees,
fed the milk of praise,
risk taking charge of this subservient universe,

even on days you wake from dreams of dread,
can't recall your name, or set a sock on straight.
For the future will astound, and your genius
dance its elegant answer; knowing despair as
understandable but not useful.

Time

From Friday-afternoon week's end helter-skelter
you took time out, to hear *Chorda Tympani;*
while sure you had no time to spend with
these student serenaders of sick children,

must invest it in chart-signing, script-writing,
xray-viewing. Yet knowing you had no more
owner's rights to time than to the four-petalled
azalea you had spied by your drive at dawn.

Nothing dreadful happened: these firefly children
took your time for free, not being *your cases.*
As you heard a voice you slowly knew was yours
stumble on refrains you thought had *gone.*

Had they more time? No, the same as you,
the students, god, the azalea. They had made
their choice, sought no grade, although you
would have given each *4.0's.* And she'd not

the least ambition for one, thoughtless of
career. That night, petals tattered, she shed
her dying shyness to the north wind, dipping

sunset eyes to you as you went in for food.

Flowers and Soldiers

An ill-timed final frost felled
my March azalea regiments;
a happening no more rational
than the child's death.

Last night they'd paraded, stems erect,
my guard of rose and crimson,
shedding their wind-jarred petal-deck
to mark my frontier posts.

Like this chosen child they'd shimmered
shortly in an early sun.
Now my nursery box brims
with their brave residue.

Their soldier paint has run to rust
in the crevices of cedar chip,
they who left without notice,
unwilling that age should wrinkle them.

Leavers and Left

At first they'd drawn near to the light of
this celestial summer camp, whooping
and winging beyond the Saturday skies,
only to race home to us with stories of
happy endings. Then to find their work here
done; time to go play in the deathless sun,
at heaven's all-night party in the firmament.

Why the young, god? Who have just
alighted here? A hard hurt, hard,
whether striking like gunshot felling
a deer at the lake's edge, or oozing
slow as air from a birthday balloon.

And where is the solace for the left,
death's chorus, wounded with the blood
of a lifetime, even as time tempers its edge?

Could it be that no child goes without
the legacy of play and song and dance
as deathless gifts to lay before us?

So that at dawn, if we listen well, gazing
from schoolroom windows at the drawing
dusk, we may hear their songs float down
to us: echoes of time's autumn chimers
exulting on their chimney stacks as we
huddle at our hearths for warmth.

Children, your mentoring, memory, aren't
wasted on us, are not wasted on us.

Rx

So you want to be healthier?
Try falling head-over-heels
in love with yourself; check yourself
in the mirror and just ask yourself:
How did I get to be so gorgeous?

Try giggling at nothing in particular,
and for no special reason that you
or anyone else can figure out,
except that your mother told you
not to. Do this *prn*[1] with unlimited refills.

Hang out with children some,
the younger the better, and best of all
ones for whom you're not
accountable. Let them call the shots
on what you all get up to.

Be downright wild, woolly and
irresponsible for a spell: rolling
downhill in the park in the rain
in your best suit might just cut it,
in company with similarly suited ones.

Have a tantrum in your car,
complete with extravagantly irreverent
gesticulations and Groucho's nose

in place; they'll be quick to shunt you
to the front at the stoplight.

Try more naps, expressly at
the downhill point of your day;
and how about doing nothing at all
for ten minutes *bid*² or *tid*,³
and doing it slowly?

Have you doodled with
paint and silly putty lately?
Fiddled in puddles, chattered in rain?
I'd be glad to write you a prescription.
Can't harm, might help.

¹*as needed;* ²*twice daily;* ³*thrice daily*